EUREKA!
THE **BIOGRAPHY** OF AN **IDEA**

CAMERA

BY LAURA DRISCOLL • ILLUSTRATED BY HECTOR BORLASCA

KANEPRESS

AN IMPRINT OF BOYDS MILLS & KANE
New York

For Gina and John —LD

To Micaela —HB

Special thanks to Susan Hacker Stang, Professor Emeritus
of Photography at Webster University and consultant for
the International Photography Hall of Fame

Kane Press
An imprint of Boyds Mills & Kane, a division of Astra Publishing House
kanepress.com
Printed in China

Library of Congress Cataloging-in-Publication Data
Names: Driscoll, Laura, author. | Borlasca, Hector, illustrator.
Title: Camera / by Laura Driscoll ; illustrated by Hector Borlasca.
Description: First edition. | New York : Kane Press, an imprint of Boyds Mills & Kane, [2021] | Series: Eureka! |
Audience: Ages 4-8. | Audience: Grades K-1. | Summary: "A nonfiction 'biography' of the camera, an everyday
object that has become ubiquitous, starting with its origins with the discovery of certain properties of light
and up through the development of the digital camera"—Provided by publisher.
Identifiers: LCCN 2020046033 (print) | LCCN 2020046034 (ebook) | ISBN 9781635924299 (paperback) |
ISBN 9781635924282 (hardcover) | ISBN 9781635924756 (ebook) Subjects: LCSH: Cameras—
History—Juvenile literature. Classification: LCC TR250 .D75 2021 (print) | LCC TR250
(ebook) | DDC 771.3—dc23 LC record available at https://lccn.loc.gov/2020046033
LC ebook record available at https://lccn.loc.gov/2020046034

10 9 8 7 6 5 4 3 2 1

PRESS A BUTTON, TAKE A PHOTO. A photograph is a moment frozen in time. Some photos are printed on paper. Some are on screens. But all photos are taken by a camera. Cameras pick up the light bouncing off people or objects.

Photos are all around us. Cameras are, too. How exactly did people figure out how to freeze time this way?

AROUND 400 BCE

About 2,500 years ago, a Chinese teacher named Mozi was in a dark room when he saw light shining through a tiny hole in a wall. The light cast the image of the world outside onto the opposite wall! One thing was particularly strange. The image was upside down and backward.

Mozi's writings about this effect are the earliest that we know of.

AROUND 350 BCE

Aristotle, a Greek thinker, noticed something similar. During a solar eclipse, sunlight shone through the gaps between tree leaves. It cast many small images of the sun onto the ground. They were all backward. *Why?* Aristotle wondered.

Light moves in a straight line. If it's squished through a small, round opening, the rays of light cross paths. When they hit a flat surface in a dark space, they reform as an upside-down, backward image.

This, very simply, is how every camera works.

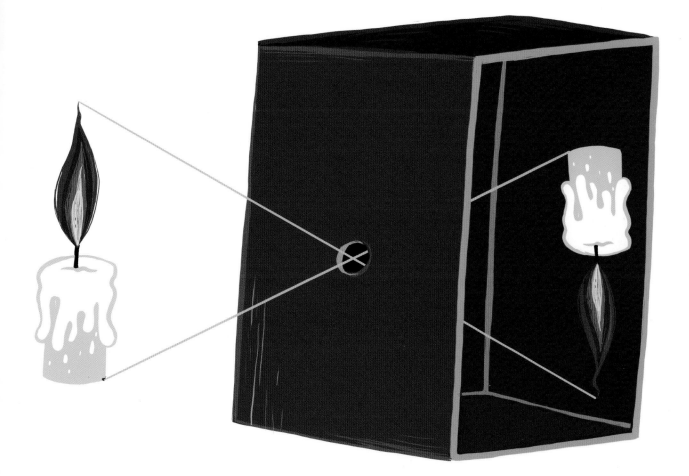

1000 CE

In Egypt, an Arab scientist named Ibn al-Haytham wanted to do experiments with light. He built a special tent with a small hole on one side. Then he hung a screen on the opposite side.

Centuries later, his invention became known as a **camera obscura** or "dark room."

1600s

In Italy, scientists made the camera obscura even better by adding a **lens**. A lens was a curved piece of glass that made the image sharper. Another Italian added a mirror. Now the light rays were flipped *again*, and the image was right-side up!

The camera obscura was used in different ways over time. Artists used it to make realistic paintings and drawings. They traced the images onto paper with pencil. Scientists also used cameras to study the sky and look at the sun safely.

1820s

Two hundred years later in France, Joseph Nicéphore Niépce coated a metal **plate** with a thin layer of asphalt, a type of tar. He put the plate inside his camera obscura. Light came in through the lens. The tar hardened wherever the light hit. Niépce left it there for hours. When he rinsed the plate, only the unhardened tar washed away. A grayish image was left behind.

1830s

Niépce's inventing partner, Louis Daguerre, tried a different type of metal plate. He coated it with different chemicals.

With these and other changes, Daguerre created a photo that could be taken in fifteen minutes. He called it the **daguerreotype**—after himself!

Now it was easier to take photos of people. But any motion made the photo blurry. And fifteen minutes was a long time to sit still—or smile.

With new lenses and better chemicals, other photographers found ways to take daguerreotypes more quickly.

1830s

Around the same time, an English scientist named William Fox Talbot slipped light-sensitive paper into his camera. He let light in through the lens. After one minute, he took the paper out and dipped it in a solution of salt. The image that appeared was a **negative**—the light areas were dark, and the dark areas were light.

Then Talbot laid this negative on top of another piece of the light-sensitive paper. The darks and lights reversed again. Unlike a daguerreotype, which was one of a kind, Talbot had created a photo that could be reprinted!

••• SAY CHEESE! •••

You are using a traditional camera to take a photo of a friend. What happens?

Light bounces off your friend and travels toward your camera. The rays pass through the camera **lens**. The lens focuses, or sharpens, the light rays before they move toward an opening, called the **aperture**.

You press the button on the camera. At that moment, a **shutter** opens. It lets the light rays through the aperture. Then the shutter closes again.

The light rays hit the **film** at the back of the camera. The film captures the light, the shadows, the colors—everything that, put together, makes a photo of your friend.

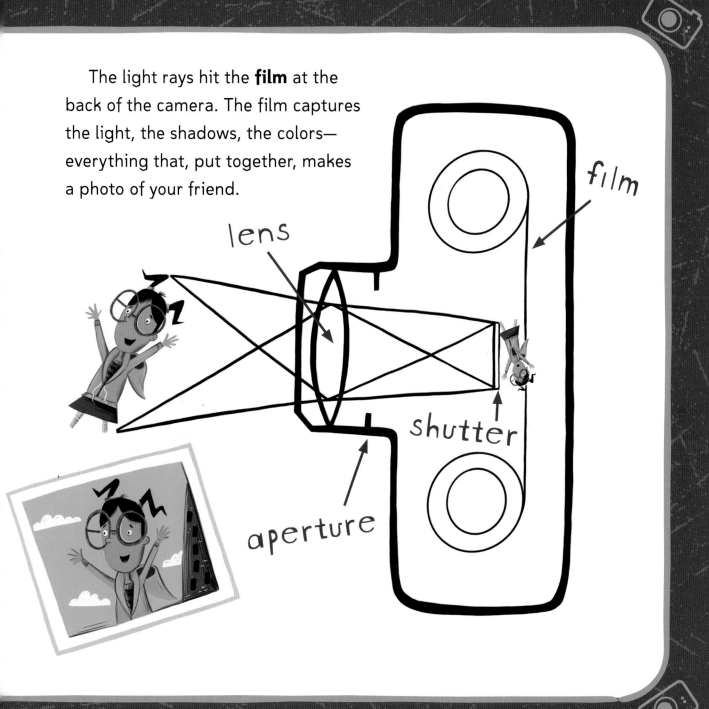

film

lens

shutter

aperture

1850s To 1870s

Instead of metal or paper, cameras now cast the images onto glass plates. The glass was coated in a chemical film that was much more sensitive to light. A new kind of shutter opened and closed in one second. Cameras didn't have to be kept steady for so long. Photographers could hold a camera in their hands.

1880s

For each photo, a new plate was loaded into the camera—until an American named George Eastman made **roll film**. He rolled up a long strip of plastic film inside the camera. After one photo was taken, a fresh part of the filmstrip was moved into place for the next photo.

Eastman invented a simple box camera called the Kodak. Inside was a roll of film for 100 photos. When the film was used up, the owner sent the camera back to the factory. The photos were printed onto paper. A factory worker loaded a new roll of film and mailed the camera and photos back to the owner.

Over the next one hundred years, cameras got smaller. Camera makers made better lenses and film. Camera prices dropped. More people could afford to take pictures.

1900

George Eastman began selling the Brownie, another box camera. It only cost $1.

1913

A German man named Oskar Barnack invented the Leica camera. It used 35mm (millimeter) film, a smaller size roll film than Eastman's.

1936

Scientists at the Eastman Kodak Company made a film that could take color photos. But color photography would not become popular and affordable for many more years.

1948

Edwin Land invented the Polaroid camera. It printed "instant photos" in about a minute.

The ideas kept coming—a lens that focused automatically, a built-in flashbulb for extra light. Taking pictures became easier and easier!

The 1980s brought a huge change—a camera without film. Instead, it had a light sensor.

When this camera takes a photo, the sensor breaks the image up into millions of pieces, or **pixels**, and measures each pixel. How bright is it? What color is it? The camera stores these measurements as numbers, or digits.

That's why these cameras are called **digital** cameras. Digital is like a language that all electronic gadgets speak. So digital photos can easily be moved from a digital camera to a computer . . .

to a printer . . .

or to a cell phone.

A digital photo can also be deleted—and new ones taken!

Today's cameras are very different from the early camera obscura. But the idea is still the same—and just as magical as ever. A camera freezes a moment in time so we can remember it, always.

••• CAMERA QUICK FACTS •••

• People take more than one trillion digital photos every year.

• At least twelve cameras remain on the moon. Astronauts needed them to take photos during moon landings, but left the cameras behind to make room in their ships for moon rocks.

• Funny cat photos date back to long before the internet! In the 1870s, an English photographer named Harry Pointer became well known for his posed photos of his cats.

• Early camera flashes were mini-explosions lit by hand. They were very dangerous!

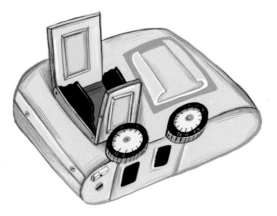

• This tiny "spy camera" made in 1957 was about the size of a matchbox.

··· CAMERA READY ···

Now the camera is in your hands! Here are tips for taking good photos.

☆ Take pictures of people or things that interest you.
☆ Move around—up high, down low, or straight on.
☆ Get up close to see the details.
☆ Try placing your subject off-center instead of right in the middle of your photo.
☆ Include bright pops of color.

What does the world look like through your camera?